Angels and Demons

The Lutheran Difference Series

Armand J. Boehme

With contributions by

Robert C. Baker

CONCORDIA PUBLISHING HOUSE • SAINT LOUIS

Copyright © 2006 by Concordia Publishing House
3558 S. Jefferson Ave., St. Louis, MO 63118-3968
1-800-325-3040 • www.cph.org

All rights reserved. Unless specifically noted, no part of this publication may be reproduced, stored in a retrieval system, or transmitted, in any form or by any means, electronic, mechanical, photocopying, recording, or otherwise, without the prior written permission of Concordia Publishing House.

Written by Armand J. Boehme

Edited by Robert C. Baker

Scripture quotations are from The Holy Bible, English Standard Version®. Copyright © 2001 by Crossway Bibles, a publishing ministry of Good News Publishers, Wheaton, Illinois. Used by permission. All rights reserved.

The quotations from the Lutheran Confessions in this publication are from *Concordia: The Lutheran Confessions*, second edition, copyright © 2006 Concordia Publishing House. All rights reserved.

This publication may be available in braille, in large print, or on cassette tape for the visually impaired. Please allow 8 to 12 weeks for delivery. Write to the Lutheran Blind Mission, 7550 Watson Rd., St. Louis, MO 63119-4409; call toll-free 1-888-215-2455; or visit the Web site: www.blindmission.org.

Manufactured in the United States of America

1 2 3 4 5 6 7 8 9 10   15 14 13 12 11 10 09 08 07 06

Contents

About This Series 4
Participant Introduction 5
Overview of Christian Denominations 6
Lutheran Facts 9
    Angels and Their Beginning 11
    Who and What Are Angels? 15
    Ranks and Number of Angels 19
    Good and Evil Angels (Demons) 23
    What Do Evil Angels Do? 27
    What Do Good Angels Do? 31
Leader Guide Introduction 35
    Answers 36
Appendix of Lutheran Teaching 60
Glossary 63

About This Series

"You believe in angels? You've got to be kidding!"
"The Bible teaches that there *are* angels . . . and demons."
"So you believe in harps, wings, pitchforks, and pointy tails?"
"Well, not exactly."

As Lutherans interact with other Christians, they often find themselves struggling to explain their beliefs and practices. Although many Lutherans have learned the "what" of the doctrines of the Church, they do not always have a full scriptural foundation to share the "why." When confronted with different doctrines, they cannot clearly state their faith, much less understand the differences.

Because of insecurities about explaining particular doctrines or practices, some Lutherans may avoid opportunities to share what they have learned from Christ and His Word. The Lutheran Difference Bible study series will identify how Lutherans differ from other Christians and use the Bible to show why Lutherans differ. These studies will prepare Lutherans to share their faith and help non-Lutherans understand the Lutheran difference.

Participant Introduction

When you hear the word *angel*, what image comes to mind? Clarence from the movie *It's A Wonderful Life*? Tess from *Touched by an Angel*? Popular culture formerly portrayed angels as harp-carrying spirits lounging on comfortable white tufts of cloud. Today, it seems, angels are all too human, such as the gritty Michael in the film by the same name or the love-starved Seth in *City of Angels*.

On the other hand, what comes to mind when you hear the words *demon* or *devil*? Hellboy from the comic book series or the movie? Various heinous creatures from *The Lord of the Rings* or *Constantine*? Or when you think about angels and demons, do you think of those comical creatures sitting on someone's shoulders—an angel in a white gown and wings on one shoulder and a demon with a pitchfork and pointy tail sitting on the other?

For many people, popular films, books, comic books, and other media are their only sources of information about angels and demons—if they believe in these creatures at all. Angels appear on screen savers, book covers, and wall calendars as pastel-colored feminine virtues or chubby, winged infants, while demons are either skulking black mists or hulks of roasted human flesh. These are inaccurate portrayals of angels and demons.

In contrast, this study will share the truth about angels and demons using God's errorless Word. What the Bible says about angels, demons, and other related topics is vitally important to Lutherans because what God says about these matters can be trusted. As God's people, we want to grow in our understanding of what God has revealed in the Scriptures, so that we believe in what God teaches us about angels and demons and can share His knowledge with others.

An Overview of Christian Denominations

The following outline of Christian history will help you understand where the different denominations come from and how they are related to one another. Use this outline in connection with the "Comparisons" sections found throughout the study. Statements of belief for the different churches were drawn from their official confessional writings.

The Great Schism

Eastern Orthodox: On July 16, 1054, Cardinal Humbert entered the Cathedral of the Holy Wisdom in Constantinople just before the worship service. He stepped to the altar and left a letter condemning Michael Cerularius, patriarch of Constantinople. Cerularius responded by condemning the letter and its authors. In that moment, Christian churches of the East and West were severed from one another. Their disagreements centered on what bread could be used in the Lord's Supper and the addition of the *filioque* statement to the Nicene Creed.

The Reformation

Lutheran: On June 15, 1520, Pope Leo X wrote a letter condemning Dr. Martin Luther for his Ninety-five Theses. Luther's theses had challenged the sale of indulgences, a fund-raising effort to pay for the building of St. Peter's Cathedral in Rome. The letter charged Luther with heresy and threatened to excommunicate him if he did not retract his writings within sixty days. Luther replied by publicly burning the letter. Leo excommunicated him on January 3 and condemned all who agreed with Luther or supported his cause.

Reformed: In 1522, the preaching of Ulrich Zwingli in Zurich, Switzerland, convinced people to break their traditional Lenten fast. Zwingli also preached that priests should be allowed to marry. When local friars challenged these departures from Medieval Church practice, the Zurich Council supported Zwingli and agreed that the Bible should guide Christian doctrine and practice. Churches of this Reformed tradition include Presbyterians and Episcopalians.

Anabaptist: In January 1525, Conrad Grebel, a follower of Ulrich Zwingli, rebaptized Georg Blaurock. Blaurock began rebaptizing others and founded the Swiss Brethren. Their insistence on adult, believers' Baptism distinguished them from other churches of the Reformation. Anabaptists attracted social extremists who advocated violence in the cause of Christ, complete pacifism, or communal living. Mennonites, Brethren, and Amish churches descend from this movement.

The Counter Reformation

Roman Catholic: When people call the Medieval Church "Roman Catholic," they make a common historical mistake. Roman Catholicism emerged after the Reformation. As early as 1518, Luther and other reformers had appealed to the pope and requested a council to settle the issue of indulgences. Their requests were hindered or denied for a variety of theological and political reasons. Finally, on December 13, 1545, thirty-four leaders from the churches who opposed the Reformation gathered at the invitation of Pope Paul III. They began the Council of Trent (1545–1563), which established the doctrine and practice of Roman Catholicism.

Post-Reformation Movements

Baptist: In 1608 or 1609, John Smyth, a former pastor of the Church of England, baptized himself by pouring water over his head. He formed a congregation of English Separatists in Holland who opposed the rule of bishops and infant baptism. This marked the start of the English Baptist churches, which remain divided doctrinally over the theology of John Calvin (Particular Baptists) and Jacob Arminius (General Baptists). In the 1800s, the Restoration Movement of Alexander Campbell, a former Presbyterian minister, adopted many Baptist teachings. These churches include the Disciples of Christ (Christian Churches) and the Churches of Christ.

Wesleyan: In 1729, John and Charles Wesley gathered with three other men to study the Scripture, receive Communion, and discipline one another according to the so-called method laid down in the Bible. Later, John Wesley's preaching caused religious revivals in England and America. Methodists, Wesleyans, Nazarenes, and Pentecostals form the Wesleyan family of churches.

Liberal: In 1799, Friedrich Schleiermacher published *Addresses on Religion* in an attempt to make Christianity appealing to people influenced by Rationalism. He argued that religion is not a body of doctrines, provable truths, or a system of ethics but belongs to the realm of feelings. His ideas did not form a new denomination but deeply influenced Christian thinking. Denominations most thoroughly affected by liberalism are the United Church of Christ, Disciples of Christ, and Unitarianism.

Lutheran Facts

All who worship the Holy Trinity and trust in Jesus Christ for the forgiveness of sins are regarded by Lutherans as fellow Christians despite denominational differences.

Lutheran churches first described themselves as *evangelische* or evangelical churches. Opponents of these churches called them *Lutheran* after Dr. Martin Luther, the sixteenth-century German Church reformer.

Lutherans are not disciples of Dr. Martin Luther, but disciples of Jesus Christ. They proudly accept the name Lutheran because they agree with Dr. Luther's teaching from the Bible, as summarized in Luther's Small Catechism.

The Lutheran Church accepts the Holy Scriptures as God's errorless Word. Because the writers of that Word, under the inspiration of the Holy Spirit, wrote about bodiless spiritual entitites created by God, Lutherans believe in angels. Good angels are spiritual beings that serve primarily as messengers (*angel* in both Hebrew and Greek means "messenger") and as ministering spirits both to God and to believers. Lutherans also believe in evil angels or demons.

Jesus' coming was foretold by angels; His conception, birth, and resurrection were announced by them. Jesus received angelic ministrations after His desert temptation and following His garden agony. He frequently encountered demon-possessed persons whom He released from satanic activity and control. Jesus preached about angels and demons. The apostles also encountered both angels and demons in their ministries. Frequently, the Bible records angels assuming bodily (corporeal) form, taking on the appearance of human men to deliver a special message from God.

Throughout the ages, the Church's creeds and her liturgies and prayers have affirmed the Bible's teaching of the existence of angels and demons. Lutherans believe that angels serve God and human beings and pray for believers. However, on the basis of Scripture, Lutherans do not condone the human worship of angels or prayers made to them. These they reserve for God alone.

To prepare for "Angels and Their Beginning," read Psalm 148:1–5.

Angels and Their Beginning

"I'm an angel."

—Irish folk-rock drummer, Caroline Corr

Claiming to be a (mostly) good or innocent person is acceptable in today's culture, even if the closest point of reference is a pure, holy spiritual being without any faults whatsoever. Such claims are prevalent especially in the public square. There, opinions about spiritual matters (and not simply God or Jesus) are so diverse that it staggers the mind. Therefore, we should not be surprised that a diversity of opinion extends to angels and demons as well. What seems to be in abundance is religious opinion; what is sorely lacking is religious fact.

1. Why do you suppose people have such diverse views about angels and demons? God and Jesus? spiritual matters in general?

The Creation of Angels

2. Read John 1:1–5 and Genesis 2:2–3. Although the Bible mentions angels in almost three hundred passages, no one passage tells us about their creation. Nevertheless, what can we conclude about the creation of angels from these two verses?

3. Read Psalm 148. What can we learn about the creation of angels from this great hymn of praise?

4. Read Colossians 1:15–17 and Nehemiah 9:6. What additional information do these verses provide about the creation and activity of the angels?

5. Luther said, "Moses writes nothing about the creation of the angels because . . . he describes only the creation of matters visible." Why do you think that in Genesis 1, God through Moses only recorded the creation of visible things, and not the creation of the invisible angels?

6. Read Acts 23:8. In Jesus' day, a Jewish religious sect called the Sadducees denied both the bodily resurrection of the dead and the existence of angels. Some people today also doubt their existence. What commandments do we break when we doubt their existence?

7. **Challenge question:** In the First Article of the Nicene Creed, when do we confess our belief in God's creation of the angels?

What Does *Angel* Mean?

The term *angel* does not designate the nature or essence of angels but rather their office as God's ambassadors or messengers. The Greek word for *angel* (*angelos*) is also used for human messengers like John the Baptist (Matthew 11:10).

8. Read Luke 1:26–38 and Matthew 28:5–8. What message did the angel Gabriel bring to Mary? What message did God's angel bring to the women on Easter Sunday?

9. Read Isaiah 6:5–7. What did the angel say to Isaiah? How did God impart forgiveness to Isaiah through the angel's ministry?

Creaturely Actions

As created beings, angels do what all of God's creatures do—worship God. They are not to be worshipped themselves, because they are created beings just like humans, although without physical bodies.

10. Read Revelation 22:8–9. What reaction did God's angel have when John fell down to worship him? What did God's angel tell John to do? What do we see angels doing in Revelation 5:11–12?

11. Read Deuteronomy 5:7 and Colossians 2:18–19. In connection to the First Commandment, why is Paul's warning to the Colossians not to be taken lightly?

Comparisons

Eastern Orthodox: "What are the *angels*? Incorporeal spirits, having intelligence, will, and power. What means the name *angel*? It means a *messenger*. Why are they so called? Because God sends them to announce his will. Thus, for instance, Gabriel was sent to announce to the Most Holy Virgin Mary the conception of the Saviour" (*The Longer Catechism of the Eastern Church*, questions 99–102).

Lutheran: "The angels in heaven pray for us, as does Christ Himself [Romans 8:34]. So do the saints on earth and perhaps also in heaven [Revelation 6:9–10]. It does not follow, though, that we should invoke and adore the angels and saints [Revelation 22:8–9]. . . . Nor should we divide different kinds of help among them, ascribing to each one a particular form of assistance, as the papists teach and do.

This is idolatry. Such honor belongs to God alone" (Smalcald Articles II 26).

Reformed/Presbyterian: "Religious worship is to be given to God, the Father, Son, and Holy Ghost; and to him alone: not to angels, saints, or any other creature: and, since the fall, not without a Mediator; nor in the mediation of any other but of Christ alone" (*The Westminster Confession of Faith*, XXI 2).

Roman Catholic: "This one only true God . . . created out of nothing, from the very first beginning of time, both the spiritual and the corporeal creature, to wit, the angelical and the mundane, and afterwards the human creature, as partaking, in a sense, of both, consisting of spirit and of body" (*Dogmatic Decrees of the Vatican Council* [Vatican I], III 1).

Baptist: "*Of the angels.* The angels were created by God to glorify him, and obey his commandments. Those who have kept their first estate he employs in ministering blessings to the heirs of salvation, and in executing his judgments upon the world" (*Confession of the Free Will Baptists*, IV 2).

Liberal: "The development of modern Christianity has been characterized by an increasing tendency to appeal to reason as a criterion of the truth . . . no element of religious faith or practice has escaped its influence . . . It is not enough that a belief, ceremony, or institution have the sanction of authority or custom; it must secure the sanction of reason by proving its truth or its worth" (Errett Gates, in *A Guide to the Study of the Christian Religion,* p. 434).

Point to Remember

"But the angel said to the women, 'Do not be afraid, for I know that you seek Jesus who was crucified. He is not here, for He has risen, as He said. Come, see the place where He lay.'" Matthew 28:5–6

To prepare for "Who and What Are Angels?" read Hebrews 1:13–14.

Who and What Are Angels?

An angel is a spiritual creature without a body created by God for the service of Christendom and the Church.

—Martin Luther

Some Christians believe that human beings turn into angels when they die. This is not true. As we learned in the first session, God created angelic beings sometime during the six days of creation. While the Bible does not give the account of the creation of angels, in two passages it does describe the creation of male and female (Genesis 1:26–27; 2:7–24). Humans, comprised of both a soul and a body, are an entirely separate order of created beings. They do not transform into angels at death.

12. Why do some believe that when people die they become angels? What comfort do you suppose they derive from such a belief?

Invisible but Present

13. Read Luke 24:39; Acts 12:7; and Hebrews 1:14. What is the nature of God's angels, and whom do they serve? How would you describe this to someone who is not a Christian?

14. Read Genesis 19:1 and Luke 1:11–12. In the Scriptures, how do angels frequently appear to believers when He wants to share a message with them? Why do you suppose this occurs?

15. Read Genesis 19:10, 15–16. What physical attributes did God give the angels that served Lot and his family?

16. Read Psalm 103:20 and 2 Thessalonians 1:7. Describe the abilities of God's good angels.

17. Read Matthew 22:30. While angels are able to do many things that human beings cannot do, what are angels unable to do as purely spiritual beings?

18. Have you or a loved one ever had what you thought was an experience with an angel? If so, and if you feel comfortable doing so, please share your experience with the group.

A Unique Angel

In the Old Testament, we read about a unique angel called "the angel of the Lord." His uniqueness is seen in what he accepts from human beings that other angels do not accept. This raises the question as to whether this angel is something more than an angel.

19. Read Judges 6:11–24. What is the Angel of the Lord called in verses 14 and 16? How does this angel react when Gideon offers divine worship (vv. 18–21)?

20. Compare Judges 13 and Isaiah 9:6. The name of the Angel of the Lord is "wonderful" (Judges 13:18). Whom did Manoah and his wife believe they had seen (v. 22)? Who is wonderful (Isaiah 9:6)?

Choir Practice

Though human beings do not become angels when they die, believing human beings have a close association with angels. That association finds expression here on earth in the Divine Service. The Divine Services are, in essence, choir practice for eternity.

21. Read 1 Corinthians 11:10 and 1 Timothy 5:21. What do these passages imply about angels and our Sunday morning worship services?

22. Read Luke 15:10. The angels rejoice whenever we repent of our sins. How may this affect how we approach confessing our sins privately to our pastor? to a neighbor we have wronged? publicly in the Divine Service?

Angelic Hymns

The Bible records the actual hymns sung by angels on earth and in heaven. See if you can determine which angelic hymns correspond to those sung in our Lutheran liturgy:

"Glory to God in the highest, and on earth peace among those with whom He is pleased!" (Luke 2:14).

"Holy, holy, holy is the LORD of hosts; the whole earth is full of His glory!" (Isaiah 6:3).

"Amen! Blessing and glory and wisdom and thanksgiving and honor and power and might be to our God forever and ever! Amen" (Revelation 7:12).

Point to Remember

"Holy, holy, holy, is the Lord God Almighty, who was and is and is to come!" Revelation 4:8

To prepare for "Ranks and Numbers of Angels," read Daniel 7:10 and Ezekiel 10:1–22.

Ranks and Numbers of Angels

The helmed Cherubim,
And sworded Seraphim,
Are seen in glittering ranks with wings display'd.

—John Milton (1608–1674), *Hymn on the Nativity*

Martin Luther once suggested that there were ten trillion angels, one thousand for each and every person on earth. Other Christians have debated the number of angels that could sit on the head of a pin. Ultimately, any speculation as to the number of angels would not reach a valid conclusion. Neither would a debate about the amount of angels in a certain location at a certain time.

23. Based on what we've already learned about angels, why is it futile to speculate about the exact number of angels that exist or that that can occupy a certain physical space at one time?

Name, Rank, and Serial Number

24. Read Deuteronomy 33:2; Job 25:2–3; Psalm 68:17; Daniel 7:10; Hebrews 12:22; and Revelation 5:11. How do these passages describe the number of angels?

25. Read Matthew 26:53. How many angels could Christ have summoned to His aid in the garden of Gethsemane? What does this imply about our Savior?

26. Read Romans 8:38–39; Ephesians 1:21; 3:10; Colossians 1:16; and 1 Peter 3:22. Some Christians find in these and other passages as many as twenty-seven ranks (divisions) of angels. Is there perhaps a better way of interpreting these passages?

27. Read Daniel 10:13; 12:2; 1 Thessalonians 4:16; and Jude 9. The Bible clearly teaches only two ranks or divisions of angels. What is the rank of the angel mentioned in these verses, and what is his name?

28. Read Isaiah 6:2–6. We meet a specific kind of angel in this passage. Describe their appearance and activities.

29. Read Genesis 3:24; Exodus 25:10–22; 26:31; 36:8. What did this kind of angel do in the Garden of Eden? How were they artistically portrayed in Moses' wilderness tabernacle?

The Throne of God

The God of Abraham, Isaac, and Jacob is King of kings and Lord of lords. It is only fitting then that He should have a throne.

30. Read 1 Samuel 4:4; 2 Kings 19:15; and Psalm 80:1; 99:1. What do these passages infer about God's throne, the mercy seat (cover) on the ark of the covenant, and the golden cherubim?

31. Read Genesis 3:24; 2 Samuel 22:11; and Psalm 18:10. According to these passages, what is the function of cherubim? What work do they perform? Why do you think God is described as riding them?

We're In Heaven

Not only were artistic representations of cherubim prominent in Moses' wilderness tabernacle, they also figured in the Jerusalem temple. These representations were highly significant of an unseen spiritual reality rarely seen by the human eye.

32. Read 1 Kings 6:23–35; 7:29–36; 2 Chronicles 3:14. Where did additional artistic depictions of cherubim appear in Solomon's temple? What is significant about these angelic representations?

33. Read Ezekiel 9:3; 10:1–22; and 11:22–23. What kind of creatures are named in these verses? What does the presence of cherubim depict?

34. Read Exodus 25:20. Why are the golden cherubim looking at the mercy seat? What did this emphasize to God's Old Testament people? What should this fact emphasize for us today?

Comparisons

Verbal Inspiration: The Holy Spirit led the prophets, evangelists, and apostles to write the books of the Bible. He guided their writing, inspiring their very words, while working through their particular styles of expression. Therefore, the Bible's words are God's Word. Conservative Christian churches hold this view. Many also maintain that the original writings of the Bible were without error (inerrancy) but that some mistakes entered the text as the scribes copied, edited, or translated the Scriptures over the centuries.

Partial Inspiration: Christians affected by theological liberalism hold different views of the inspiration of the Bible. For example, some would assert that the Bible is God's Word but that the authors erred in some factual details. Others would say that the Bible contains God's Word and that the Spirit leads people today to determine which parts of the Bible God wants them to follow. Still others would say that the Bible is one testimony to God's Word along with writings used in other religions.

Inspired Translations: Some churches hold that God inspired certain translations of the Bible. For example, the Eastern Orthodox Church holds that the Greek Septuagint translation of the Old Testament was inspired by God. Some English-speaking Protestants hold that God inspired the King James translation of the Bible.

Point to Remember

"Then I looked, and I heard around the throne and the living creatures and the elders the voice of many angels, numbering myriads of myriads and thousands of thousands." Revelation 5:11

To prepare for "Good and Evil Angels (Demons)," read Matthew 4:1–11.

Good and Evil Angels (Demons)

The road to hell is paved with adverbs.

—Author Stephen King

None of us will arrive in hell by selecting the wrong words for a horror novel. However, most of us can recall having taken a wrong road and ending up in the wrong place. Most of the time, our travel stories have a happy ending. However, sometimes travelers are not able to get back on the right road. A wrong road leads to a place of great danger, and before they realize it, it is too late.

35. Describe the time or times you've taken a wrong turn and ended up on the wrong road. Were you able to get back on the right road? What helped you get there?

Which Road?

God's created angels faced a fork in the road. Everything was going fine until that point.

36. Read Genesis 28:11–13; Psalm 103:20–21; and John 1:50–51. According to these passages, what are some additional activities of God's good angels?

37. Read Genesis 1:31 and 3:1. When God says that everything that He created was "very good," what does that say about *all* the angels God created? When might that have changed?

38. Read Isaiah 14:12–15, Ezekiel 28:12–19; 31:1–17. What elements in these passages depict Satan's fall from heaven?

39. Read Jude 6 and Revelation 12:4. Describe the wrong road taken by some of God's good angels.

40. Job 1:6–7, 2:1–2, 7; Mark 5:12–13; and Matthew 12:43–44. Prior to Christ's ascent into heaven, the devil and his evil angels were allowed into God's presence in heaven. Where are they now?

41. Read Matthew 6:13. In the Lord's Prayer, we asked that God deliver us from evil. How is this accomplished?

The Right Road

The above passages show that God's angels were faced with the decision to either go off on the wrong road with Satan or stay on the right road with God, their Creator. The following passages strongly emphasize this truth.

42. Read Matthew 18:10. What benefit do the elect angels now enjoy?

43. Read 1 Timothy 5:21. Describe the state and condition of God's good angels.

The Wrong Road

The good angels remained on the right road, but some angels did not, including Satan. The world has never been the same since.

44. Read John 8:44 and 1 Timothy 3:6. In what did Satan no longer abide? What caused that? In other words, what was the devil's original sin? Discuss this in reference to Romans 1.

45. Read 2 Peter 2:4 and Matthew 25:41. What was the result of the fall of the evil angels, including Satan? What will be their final abode?

Comparisons

Many philosophical ideas compete for our attention when we discuss biblical concepts like angels and demons. Often Bible readers are not even aware that such ideas influence and color their interpretation of God's Word.

Rationalism: "We can figure that out." Rationalism rejects religious faith or dogma in determining truth and relies solely on human reason and analysis. Secular Humanism, which deifies the human person, human society, and its achievements, and atheism, which denies that God exists, are philosophically related to Rationalism. Rationalists would deny the existence of angels and demons because the concept of invisible, bodiless beings is irrational.

Relativism: "Everything is relative." There is no absolute reference for the values human beings place in their beliefs or behaviors. As a philosophical theory, relativism has two inherent problems: either it is itself relativistic (that is, subject to change) or absolutist (by claiming there are no absolutes). Relativists would allow for multiple and competing authorities or sources of information about angels and demons besides the Bible.

Subjectivism: "Perception creates reality." There is no true reality apart from our perception. Objectivists, however, argue that there is an underlying reality to all things existing independently of our perception. Subjectivists would tend to base what they believe about angels and demons not on external sources of authority but on their own personal experience or feelings.

Point to Remember

"In the presence of God and of Christ Jesus and of the elect angels, I charge you to keep these rules without prejudging, doing nothing from partiality." 1 Timothy 5:21

To prepare for "What Do Evil Angels Do?" read Matthew 4:1–11.

What Do Evil Angels Do?

The devil made me do it.

–Comedian Clerow "Flip" Wilson (1933–1998)

It seems human interest in the devil and evil in general sometimes takes a comedic twist, which is here exemplified by the catch phrase coined by the late Flip Wilson. However, in reality there is nothing funny about the devil. He is very real. Demons are very real. Demonic possession is very real. And perhaps this is one of the devil's better tricks. By dulling our senses to the real danger he and his minions pose, we may be more willing to take the bait.

46. Why do some people downplay the danger associated with following one's horoscope, experimenting with witchcraft or Wicca, participating in pagan religious rites, or playing with a Ouija board?

The Results of Their Revolt

The fall of Satan and the evil angels had consequences for the human race. They seek to draw as many of us as possible into their rejection of our heavenly Father's Word and His grace.

47. Read Genesis 3:1–13; Luke 8:12; and 1 Timothy 4:1–3. Discuss the steps taken by the devil in tempting Eve and Adam, and the relationship between temptation and God's Word.

48. Read Genesis 3:14–24 and John 8:44. What has the devil's rebellion and the revolt of the evil angels brought into this world?

49. Read Job 1:13–22; 2:7; Luke 13:11–16; and 2 Corinthians 12:7. What evils brought about by Satan and his evil angels are noted in these passages?

50. Read Matthew 2:13–18; 4:1–11; John 13:2; and 2 Corinthians 11:13–15. What steps did the devil take in attempting to thwart our salvation in Christ? What steps does he take today?

51. Read Zechariah 3:1–2 and Revelation 12:7–12. The devil is a liar, murderer, deceiver, and a tempter. Now that Christ has come in the flesh, what is the devil's status now as an accuser of believers?

52. Read Deuteronomy 18:10–14; Jeremiah 27:9–10; Galatians 5:19–21; Revelation 21:8; 22:15. Discuss how you might use these passages in discouraging someone from participating in the occult.

Their Possession of People

Many have discounted demonic possession as an old wives' tale or something from a less enlightened age. But demonic possession was real in Jesus' day, and it is still real today.

53. Read Mark 5:1–20; 9:17–29; John 13:2; Acts 16:16–17. Describe some of the infirmities caused by demons in possessed persons.

54. Read Mark 1:23–28; Luke 4:40–41; and Hebrews 2:14–18. What did Jesus do for the demon-possessed individuals brought to Him? How does He help us as we wrestle with sin and evil in our lives?

Their Torment in Hell

Sinful human beings may be led by God's Spirit through God's Word to genuine repentance and faith in Christ. They will spend an eternity in a new heaven and a new earth. There is no such hope for the sinful angels who rebelled against God. The devil and his cohorts will spend an eternity in hell.

55. Read Matthew 13:36–50 and Revelation 20:11–15. What will be the fate of all who die without faith in Christ? What is the Church's life-giving message to the world until Christ's return (Acts 2:38–39)?

56. Read Matthew 8:29; 25:41; and Revelation 20:10. What is the end of the devil and all his evil angels? How will they spend eternity?

Our God-given Victory

The sword of the Spirit is God's Word. Here are powerful Bible passages to help you when you are assaulted by the devil:

"No temptation has overtaken you that is not common to man. God is faithful, and He will not let you be tempted beyond your ability, but with the temptation He will also provide the way of escape, that you may be able to endure it" (1 Corinthians 10:13).

"But thanks be to God, who gives us the victory through our Lord Jesus Christ" (1 Corinthians 15:57).

"The Lord will rescue me from every evil attack and will bring me safely to His heavenly kingdom. To Him be glory forever and ever. Amen" (2 Timothy 4:18).

"Submit yourselves therefore to God. Resist the devil, and he will flee from you" (James 4:7).

"Be sober-minded; be watchful. Your adversary the devil prowls around like a roaring lion, seeking someone to devour. Resist him, firm in your faith, knowing that the same kinds of suffering are being experienced by your brotherhood throughout the world" (1 Peter 5:8–9).

"Little children, you are from God and have overcome them, for He [Jesus] who is in you is greater than he who is in the world" (1 John 4:4).

Point to Remember

"The reason the Son of God appeared was to destroy the works of the devil." 1 John 3:8

To prepare for "What Do Good Angels Do?" read Matthew 18:10.

What Do Good Angels Do?

To serve and to protect.
–Common law enforcement motto

Sometimes the motto "To serve and to protect" is emblazoned on police cars or cruisers. The motto serves to emphasize that the police are to serve citizens in time of need and to protect them from criminals and evildoers. In the same way, God created His holy angels to serve Him and His people. Now they also protect His people against the evil one and his evil angels.

57. How often are we aware of the care and protection given us by the police or other public servants? Why might we be unaware of all the things they do for us?

Servants of the Most High

Like our police forces, good angels are God's servants to carry out His will both in heaven and upon earth. And like our police forces, some of their duties are pleasant, while others are difficult. This is especially the case when it comes to restraining and punishing evil.

58. Read Genesis 19:1–3, 10–12, 15–16; Daniel 6:19–22; Acts 5:12–21. In these passages, how did angels serve God's people? How do they deliver us from evil today (Hebrews 1:13–14)?

59. Read Genesis 19:13, 23–28; Acts 12:20–23; Revelation 20:1–3. While the duties of God's angels described in these passages may

surprise us, how do angels protect God's people by restraining or punishing evildoers?

60. Read Matthew 1:20–21; Mark 1:13; Luke 22:39–43. How did angels serve and protect Jesus while He was on earth? Try to recall other passages where angels appear during Jesus' earthly ministry.

61. Read Acts 1:10–11; 8:26–40; 10:21–33. How did angels also serve and protect the apostles as they went forth teaching and baptizing?

62. Read Zechariah 1:7–17; Luke 24:1–6; Revelation 1:1–3. As we learned earlier, *angel* means "messenger." From these verses, describe other important messages God's angels have brought to people.

63. Read Psalm 103:19–21; Hebrews 1:1–6; Revelation 5:11–14. Having seen how God's holy angels serve Him on earth, how do they serve God in heaven?

Companions of God's People

As they serve us, God's angels are our companions here on earth. The elect angels do what they were created to do—God's will. Christians have been given the gift of faith so that we can serve God. Angels help us to do that.

64. Read 1 Corinthians 4:9; Ephesians 3:8–11; 1 Peter 1:10–12. Angels are very interested in the life of the Church on earth. In what do they have particular interest?

65. Read Hebrews 13:2. What do we at times do for angels? How should this affect how we treat strangers? those who are less fortunate?

Protectors of the Saints

God's holy angels are present as we worship. They pray for us. They observe the struggles of our lives. They help us. God's angels guard and protect us our whole lives.

66. Read Matthew 18:10 and Luke 16:22. What do angels continue to do for us while we live? What do they do for us when we die? Describe what this means for you personally.

67. Read Matthew 24:31; 1 Corinthians 6:3; Revelation 7:9–17. What will angels do for believers on the Last Day? What will believers do for angels? Discuss our glorious and joyous future together beginning with the return of Christ on the Last Day.

Angelic Appearances and Jesus

Below is a list of angelic appearances during our Lord's ministry upon earth, beginning with the announcement of His birth and concluding with the angels' appearance following His ascension into heaven.

The angel Gabriel announces the conception and birth of Jesus to the Virgin Mary.	Luke 1:26–38
An angel encourages Joseph to care for Mary and her unborn, holy Child.	Matthew 1:20–21
The angel and the angelic multitude announce the birth of Jesus to the shepherds.	Luke 2:8–14
An angel warns Joseph to take Mary and the baby Jesus into Egypt.	Matthew 2:13
An angel informs Joseph that it is safe to return with Mary and Jesus to Nazareth.	Matthew 2:19–20
Angels minister to Jesus after His temptation by the devil in the wilderness.	Matthew 4:11; Mark 1:13
An angel ministers to Jesus in the garden of Gethsemane.	Luke 22:39-43
Two angels converse with Mary Magdalene, Johanna, Mary the mother of James, and Salome about the bodily resurrection of Jesus.	Matthew 28:1–7; Mark 16:1–7; Luke 24:1–7
Two angels appear to Mary Magdalene prior to Jesus' appearance to her.	John 20:11–14
Two angels speak to the disciples following Jesus' ascension into heaven.	Acts 1:10–11

Point to Remember

"But you have come to Mount Zion and to the city of the living God, the heavenly Jerusalem, to an innumerable company of angels in festal gathering, and to the assembly of the firstborn who are enrolled in heaven." Hebrews 12:22–23

Leader Guide

Leaders, please note the different abilities of your class members. Some will easily find the many passages listed in this study. Others will struggle to find even the easy passages. To help everyone participate, team up members of the class. For example, if a question requires that you look up several passages, assign one passage to one group, the second to another, and so on. Divide up the work. Let participants present the different answers they discover.

Each topic is divided into four easy-to-use sections.

Focus: key concepts that will be discovered.

Inform: guides the participants into Scripture to uncover truth concerning a doctrine.

Connect: enables participants to apply that which is learned in Scripture to their lives and provide them an opportunity to formulate and articulate a defense of a key doctrine.

Vision: provides participants with practical suggestions for extending the theme of the lesson out of the classroom and into the world.

Angels and Their Beginning

Objectives

By the power of the Holy Spirit working through God's Word, participants will (1) believe that God created angels, (2) understand that angels are God's messengers, and (3) recognize that as God's creatures, angels are not to be worshipped.

Opening Worship

The hymn "At the Name of Jesus" (*LSB* 512; *LW* 178) speaks about God's creation of angels (stanza 2) and the presence of angels on the Last Day (stanza 6). Another hymn that could be used is "Lord God, to Thee We All Give Praise" (*LSB* 522; *LW* 189; *TLH* 254).

Prayer: O everlasting God, whose wise planning has ordained and constituted the ministry of men and angels in a wonderful order, mercifully grant that, as your holy angels always serve you in heaven, so by your appointment they may also help and defend us here on earth; through Jesus Christ, your Son, our Lord, who lives and reigns with you and the Holy Spirit, one God, now and forever. Amen.

Focus

1. Answers will vary. Diverse opinions about spiritual matters, including God, Jesus, angels, and demons, arise because people rely on their own human reason or experience as the sources of authority instead of God's Word. Human reason, unaided by faith, is totally blind to the truth of spiritual matters. It creates for itself a self-made and self-serving religion. For example, some believe that angels and demons either do not exist or, if they do, they are harmless (angels) or will only hurt the other guy or gal (demons).

The Creation of Angels (Inform)

2. While nearly three hundred Bible passages mention angels, Genesis 1 is silent about their creation. However, John 1:1–3 informs us that before God created the universe, nothing existed besides Him. Also, Genesis 2:2–3 shows that God rested from all His creative work on the seventh day. From these two passages, we learn that God created angelic beings sometime during the six days God created "all that is seen and unseen," as we confess in the Nicene Creed. Those who doubt that God created angels at all, finding no mention of them in Genesis 1, should direct themselves to passages where Jesus, God in human flesh, confirms their existence (see Matthew 22:30; 25:31; and Luke 16:22).

3. Psalm 148 begins with the Hebrew word *Hallelujah*, meaning "Praise the Lord." This psalm depicts all of God's creation singing a great hymn of praise to its Creator God. Note how "angels" and "hosts" (v. 2) are included with "heavens," "heights" (v. 1), "sun," "moon," and "stars" (v. 3), indeed with everything else that God created. The implication is clear: God created angels.

4. Colossians 1:15–17 affirms what we learned from John 1:1–5, namely, that the preincarnate Son of God, along with the Father and the Holy Spirit, was active in creating all that was made. This includes angels. Nehemiah 9:6 teaches that God created the host of heaven, which worships Him. Angels are called "the host of heaven" (1 Kings 22:19) or the "heavenly host" (Luke 2:13). Therefore, part of angelic activity is to worship the triune God—Father, Son, and Holy Spirit.

5. Answers may vary. In one of his table talks, Luther said that he thought God did not describe the creation of invisible angels because God did not want people to speculate about it.

6. Denying angels' existence breaks the First Commandment, because such denial exalts human reason above God; the Second Commandment, because it besmirches the holiness of God's Word and calls Christ a liar; the Third Commandment, because it contravenes God's Word, the exact opposite of holding it sacred and gladly hearing and learning it; and the Eighth Commandment, because it doubts God's Word and accuses God of being untruthful.

7. The First Article of the Nicene Creed confesses God as "maker of . . . all things visible and invisible," including angelic beings. The Creed reflects not only the scriptural truth concerning God's creation of the angels, but also the source of our forgiveness of sins, including the

sin of disbelief in angels, which is found in the Second Article: "And in one Lord Jesus Christ . . . who for us men and for our salvation."

What Does *Angel* Mean? (Connect)

8. The angel Gabriel told the Virgin Mary that she would conceive and give birth to the Messiah, the "Son of God" (Luke 1:35), whom God had promised in the Old Testament Scriptures. Following Jesus' crucifixion and burial, the angel's message to the women at the tomb was that Jesus had risen as He said and that they should announce this fact to His disciples (Matthew 28:6–7).

9. Isaiah 6:1–8 offers a beautiful portrait of Confession and Absolution. Seeing God in His temple, the prophet Isaiah is moved to confess his guilt in God's awesome and holy presence. Through the actions of the angel, God broke the barrier between Himself and Isaiah and forgave Isaiah's sin. The seraph, a type of winged angel, took a burning coal from the altar of sacrifice, pointing to the atonement secured by the shedding of blood. The angel's message of reconciliation ("Behold, this has touched your lips; your guilt is taken away, and your sin atoned for" [Isaiah 6:7]) brought God's forgiveness personally to Isaiah. This Absolution moved the prophet, and enabled Him to powerfully preach to God's people concerning the coming Christ (Isaiah 7:14).

Creaturely Actions (Vision)

10. The angel rejected John's worship and pointed to his common servanthood with John and the prophets. He clearly exhorted John to "Worship God" (Revelation 22:8–9). Worshiping God alone is what all of God's creatures do—whether they are invisible angels or visible human beings.

11. The First Commandment (Deuteronomy 5:7) forbids the worship of anyone or any thing other than the triune God. Paul's warning applies to us as well. While portraits, paintings, statues, and special days such as St. Michael and All Angels remind us of God's special messengers, we should still never worship or pray to angel. Since all people are sinners whether they worship angels or not, we all need God's grace and forgiveness in Christ. That grace enables us to join the angelic choirs of heaven in singing their songs of praise to Father, Son, and Holy Spirit.

Who and What Are Angels?

Objectives

By the power of the Holy Spirit working through God's Word, participants will (1) learn that human beings do not become angels when they die, (2) understand more about the Angel of the Lord, and (3) rejoice that church services are choir practice for singing with the angelic choirs of heaven.

Opening Worship

The Gloria in Excelsis (*LSB*, p. 154; *LW*, p. 138), either hymn of praise (*LW*, pp. 160–163), the Sanctus (*LSB*, p. 161; *LW*, pp. 170–171), or the Te Deum could be used (*LSB* 223–225; *LW* 8). Another liturgical hymn would be "Isaiah, Mighty Seer, in Spirit Soared" (*LSB* 960; *LW* 214; *TLH* 249). Hymns that emphasize humans joining angelic choirs are "Holy God, We Praise Thy Name" (*LSB* 940; *LW* 171), "The Bridegroom Soon Will Call Us" (*LSB* 514; *LW* 176), "Wake, Awake, for Night Is Flying" (*LSB* 516; *LW* 177), "Behold a Host Arrayed in White" (*LSB* 676; *LW* 192), "Lord Jesus Christ, Be Present Now" (*LSB* 902; *LW* 201), and "God Himself Is Present" (*LSB* 907; *LW* 206).

Prayer: Lord God, heavenly Father, we thank You for creating Your holy angels to serve those whom you saved by the Gospel of Your beloved Son. Pardon our sins, especially where we have doubted Your angelic help. Bless us with the righteousness of Christ our Savior as we study Your Word. In Jesus' name. Amen.

Focus

12. Answers may vary. Perhaps some people do not understand, or do not believe in, the Bible's teaching about the bodily resurrection of the dead. Others may misunderstand Matthew 22:30 in which Jesus states believers are "like the angels in heaven," such as, in heaven males and females do not marry (as angels are unmarried). Some may misread that text, missing the words *like* or *as* and think that believers become angels

when they die and go to heaven. More comforting than the misguided notion that believers become angels when they die is the Scriptural truth that at death the souls of believers join the angels and saints with God and Christ in heaven, looking forward to the bodily resurrection of the dead.

Invisible But Present (Inform)

13. Angels are spiritual creatures—creatures without physical, touchable, seeable bodies (Luke 24:39). While they do not occupy space and are not present in all places at the same time (omnipresent), they nevertheless may be at a particular place (e.g., Peter was visited by an angel in prison in Acts 12:7). Angels are "ministering spirits" (Hebrews 1:14) who serve "those who inherit salvation" by being believers. This is one of the links between angels and the Gospel that saves sinners and enables them to inherit eternal life and salvation. God's good angels serve Christians—those saved by God's grace in Christ.

14. Genesis 19:1 tells us that angels can assume bodily form, for these angels were seen by Lot and by many other men in town who wanted to have sex with them (Genesis 19:5). In Luke 1:11–12, God's Word tells us that an angel of the Lord appeared to Zechariah in the temple and that Zechariah saw the angel.

15. God's Word tells us that the angels in their assumed physical bodies "reached out their hands and brought Lot into the house with them and shut the door" (Genesis 19:10). The angels also took the hands of Lot his wife and daughters and pulled them out of Sodom so they would not be destroyed therein (vv. 15–16). Thus, although they do not possess physical bodies, God can provide angels with the ability to act as if they had bodies, including the physical attributes of dimension, touch, and strength.

16. God's angels are "mighty ones" (Psalm 103:20; 2 Thessalonians 1:7). However, God's Word does not say that angels are almighty in the same way that God is almighty. Whatever God-given gifts and abilities they possess, angels remain created beings subject to God. They are subordinate to God's power and Christ's rule (1 Peter 3:22).

17. Jesus says that angels do not experience marriage (Matthew 22:30), because they are spiritual creatures without bodies. Lacking the physical bodies of human beings today, angels cannot procreate. Hence, unlike human beings, all the angels that exist now were created sometime within the six days of creation. Since human beings do not become an-

gels when they die, and since angels do not have little angel children, their numbers do not increase.

This verse also puts to rest the speculation some have concerning Genesis 6:2. Some believe on the basis of this verse that angels (their faulty interpretation of the phrase "sons of God") married human beings and had half-angel, half-human children or even giants. The context rules out this faulty interpretation for it speaks only of human beings. Genesis 6:1 speaks of "man" and "daughters." The idea that angels married human women and had giant children with them is fiction.

18. Answers may vary. As Lutheran Christians, we want to be sensitive to those who may have had an experience with an angel. On one hand, we do not want to flatly deny that such experiences can occur even today. (This is not Christianity, but rationalism, which completely denies the supernatural; see Hebrews 13:2.). However, we should neither look for such experiences nor expect them to occur as part of our lives on earth. We should also exercise caution in this matter, since Satan can appear as an "angel of light" (2 Corinthians 11:14). Rather, we should look to Jesus, "the founder and perfecter of our faith" (Hebrews 12:2), who in His flesh exercises power and dominion over angels (1 Peter 3:22).

A Special "Angel" (Connect)

19. The Angel of the Lord is also called "the LORD" (Judges 6:14, 16, 23). Gideon is told he will not die even though he has seen the Lord face-to-face. Unless special dispensation is granted, no sinful human being can see God face-to-face and live (Exodus 33:20–23). What the Angel accepts from Gideon is divine worship in the form of a sacrifice (vv. 18–21).

20. Having seen the Angel of the Lord, Manoah said, "We shall surely die, for we have seen God!" (Judges 13:22). Manoah's wife assured him that that would not be the case since the Angel had accepted their sacrifice and had made them a special promise. Angels are created beings, are not to be worshipped (Revelation 22:9), and sacrifices are not to be made to them. Therefore, since this Angel accepts the worship and sacrifice of Gideon, Manoah, and his wife, He must be God. Otherwise, the First Commandment is being broken. Older orthodox Lutheran theologians like Johann Gerhard believed that the Angel in this appearance was the preincarnate Christ. Other orthodox commentators maintain that not every reference of "the angel of the Lord" is to be interpreted as a manifestation of the preincarnate Christ, the second Person of the Holy

Trinity, but are, nevertheless, theophanies, which are manifestations of God.

Choir Practice (Vision)

21. On the basis of 1 Corinthians 11:10 and 1 Timothy 5:21, Lutheran theologians such as Heinrich Schmid and R. C. H. Lenski have said that God's angels worship with us here on earth. Better put, in our Sunday Divine Services, we join with the angels in their heavenly worship. This is also implied in the Christian liturgy when the pastor prays, "Therefore with angels and archangels and with all the company of heaven we laud and magnify your glorious name, evermore praising you and saying, 'Holy, holy, holy Lord, God of Sabaoth. Heav'n and earth are full of your glory." (*LSB*, p. 195; *TLH*, p. 25–26).

22. God's angels in heaven rejoice when one sinner repents. Whenever we confess our sins and receive the forgiveness of our sins through Christ's Gospel, there is great joy among the heavenly host. We should approach confessing our sins either privately or publicly not with a sullen demeanor, but in the full confidence that because of Christ's death and resurrection, our sins have been fully atoned. We are forgiven!

Ranks and Number of Angels

Objectives

By the power of the Holy Spirit working through God's Word, participants will (1) understand there are an infinite number of angels, (2) see that angels are divided into basically two ranks—angels and archangels, and (3) gain insight into the symbolism of God's cherubim.

Opening Worship

Consider singing "Ye Watchers and Ye Holy Ones" (*LSB* 670; *LW* 308), "Let All Mortal Flesh Keep Silence" (*LSB* 621; *LW* 241), "Up Through Endless Ranks of Angels" (*LSB* 491; *LW* 152), or "He Whom Shepherds Once Came Praising" (*LW* 54).

Prayer: We implore you, O Lord, to pour forth your grace on us that, as we have known the incarnation of your Son, Jesus Christ, by the message of the angel, so by His cross and Passion we may be brought to the glory of His resurrection; through our Lord Jesus Christ, who lives and reigns with you and the Holy Spirit, one God, now and forever. Amen.

Focus

23. Answers may vary. It is impossible to know the number of angels that exist because Scripture does not tell us. Also, the discussion about the number of angels that could stand on the head of a pin would be futile because angels are spiritual, illocal creatures that occupy no physical space.

Name, Rank, and Serial Number (Inform)

24. **Deuteronomy 33:2**—"The ten thousands of holy ones." **Job 25:2–3**—"Is there any number to His armies?" **Psalm 68:17**—"The chariots of God are twice ten thousand, thousands upon thousands." **Daniel 7:10**—"A thousand thousands served him [God], and ten thousand times ten thousand stood before him." **Hebrews 12:22**—"But you

have come . . . to innumerable angels in festal gathering." **Revelation 5:11**—"And I heard . . . the voice of many angels, numbering myriads of myriads and thousands of thousands."

25. In Jesus' day, the word *legion* designated a Roman military band of about six thousand soldiers. Thus, Jesus is noting that His Father could summon to His aid more than seventy-two thousand angels. This speaks not only to the immense number of angels but also to the intimate relationship that Jesus, God's only-begotten Son, enjoys with His Father.

26. Some Early Church Fathers, and even some Lutheran theologians, believed that these passages indicated numerous ranks or divisions of angels. While the word *angel* appears in Romans 8:38–39 and *angels* appears in 1 Peter 3:22, the other terms in these passages could refer either to (a) angels as a whole, (b) fallen angels, or (c) earthly powers active against Christ's Church. (In Ephesians 6:21, Paul uses the phrase "angels, authorities, and powers" to refer to "spiritual forces of *evil* in the heavenly realms" without implying that ranks exist among demons.) Thus, these passages are perhaps best interpreted as referring to all angels, not different ranks of angels. Cherubim and seraphim are specific names for certain types of angels, not angelic ranks.

27. The only clear ranking the Bible speaks about in relationship to angels is the distinction between "angels" and "archangels." Daniel 10:13 and 12:1 describe Michael as "the great prince" or as "one of the chief princes." 1 Thessalonians 4:16 speaks about an "archangel," which Jude 9 identifies as Michael. From these verses, we can conclude that Michael is the only archangel.

28. Isaiah 6:2–6 is the only passage in the Bible mentioning a type of angel called seraphim. Here they are standing above God, who is seated on His heavenly throne. The seraphim possess—according to this text—faces, feet, and six wings each. One of the seraphim acts in response to Isaiah's statement about his sin. Acting much as a human priest would, the angel uses tongs to remove a hot coal from the altar and touches Isaiah's lips with it. The Absolution is clear: "Your guilt is taken away, and your sin atoned for" (v. 7).

29. **Genesis 3:24**—We first encounter another kind of angel: the cherubim. This occurs after the fall in the Garden of Eden. While in popular art cherubs are often depicted as chubby babies with wings, the first ones we meet in the Bible are fearsome spiritual creatures brandishing flaming weaponry. **Exodus 25:19–22; 26:31; 36:8**—The artistic depictions of cherubim appear in the Moses' wilderness tabernacle and

later the Jerusalem temple. Apparently, while the seraphim possess three pairs of wings, the cherubim possess only one pair.

Look Where I Am (Connect)

30. All these verses speak of God being enthroned above the cherubim. This designation reflects the design of the top of the ark of the covenant. It was above the ark's mercy seat and in between the two cherubim that God would come to meet and speak with His people (Exodus 25:22). The mercy seat was an earthly symbol of God's gracious and merciful presence in the midst of His people. It was also a symbol of God's heavenly throne and of God's kingly rule over His people. God's heavenly throne, seen in Isaiah 6, is surrounded by angels. So the symbol of His throne here on earth, the mercy seat, is surrounded by angels as well.

31. **Genesis 3:24**—The cherubim with their flaming swords prevented sinners from entering the Garden of Eden after the fall, thus keeping impenitent sinners from having an eternal sinful existence resulting from eating the fruit of the tree of life. These cherubim exhibited God's wrath over sin. **2 Samuel 22:11; Psalm 18:10**—These passages note that God rides on a cherub and flies in this manner. Answers will vary as to why. God's riding on cherubim as a king rides in his chariot is again a reference to the ark. The ark was a visible manifestation of God's presence, His enthronement between the two cherubim, and above the atonement cover (lid), or mercy seat of the ark.

We're In Heaven (Vision)

32. In addition to the golden cherubim on the mercy seat of the ark of the covenant and woven into the curtain separating the Most Holy Place from the Holy Place, Solomon's temple had additional representations of these angelic creatures. On either side of the ark, Solomon placed two large cherubim (fifteen feet tall each and each with a fifteen-foot wingspan) crafted of olive wood. Cherubim were also carved into the temple walls and on the temple doors and graced the portable bronze carts used by the priests for ceremonial washing. As these angels truly surround God's heavenly throne, so they were visible around His spiritual throne and seat of mercy here on earth. The tabernacle and the temple signified God's gracious and merciful presence in the midst of His people.

33. In Ezekiel, we see the cherubim that surround God's throne. Their presence around the throne of God is symbolized by the cherubim seen in the temple and tabernacle. Ezekiel is commanded by God to record the fact that God's presence and glory left the temple because of the idolatry and sin of the Israelites. As Hebrews 9:5 notes, these angels are "cherubim of glory." Their presence either in reality or in symbolic form reflected the presence of God and of His glory. When God's glory departed the Jerusalem temple, so did the living cherubim (Ezekiel 10:18–19; 11:22–23). Truly God's people could see the cherubim carved in the temple walls and conclude that if God's angels are here, then God is here also, and therefore I must be in the presence of God. Significantly, cherubim appear in Ezekiel's idealized temple (Ezekiel 41:18–25) to which God's glory returns (Ezekiel 43).

34. The cherubim constantly gaze at the mercy seat of the ark of the covenant. This is God's throne and the place of His gracious and merciful presence on earth. The blood sprinkled there atoned for the sins of the people (Leviticus 16:6, 11, 14–17). The cherubim look at blood sprinkled by the Jewish high priest once a year, which looks forward in time to another, final sacrifice and another High Priest. Indeed, as Paul says, Jesus, our Savior, is God's mercy seat (Greek: *hilasterion*; Romans 3:25), the full manifestation of God's presence, and the only place from whence we receive the full forgiveness of sins, pardon, peace, and eternal life. The eyes of the cherubim, and our eyes, are turned to God's mercy seat, God's throne of grace, Jesus, our Lord. There we contemplate in deepest humility and adoration God's unfathomable love in Christ for sinners, like you and I. Amen.

Good and Evil Angels (Demons)

Objectives

By the power of the Holy Spirit working through God's Word, participants will (1) understand that all angels were created good, (2) that some sinned and fell away from their created purpose, and (3) that some remained good and are now confirmed in their goodness.

Opening Worship

These hymns could be used for the opening devotion since they either mention by name both good and bad angels, the devil, or include the bad angels in phrases such as the powers of hell, and so on. You could sing "A Mighty Fortress Is Our God" (*LSB* 656; *LW* 298), "We Walk in Danger All the Way" (*LW* 391), "Now Rest Beneath Night's Shadow" (*LSB* 880; *LW* 485), or "Onward Christian Soldiers" (*LSB* 662; *LW* 518).

Prayer: Dear heavenly Father, through the death of Your Son You have destroyed sin and death, and by His glorious resurrection You have brought life and immortality to light. By the power and might of your holy angels, deliver and protect us from the assaults of the devil and his evil angels. Help us to trust in the protection You grant to us through Your holy angels. We ask this through Christ, our Lord. Amen.

Focus

35. Answers may vary. All of us have either misinterpreted directions, misunderstood road signs, or have been given wrong information when trying to find our destination. Allow participants to share their experiences taking the wrong road.

Which Road? (Inform)

36. **Genesis 28:11–13; John 1:50–51**—Both of these passages indicate that angels pass between heaven and earth as if they were ascending and descending a ladder or a stairway. Participants should keep in

mind that angels are illocal, that is, as spiritual beings they do not occupy space, and that the revealed image of a ladder or stairway is perhaps the most the finite human mind can handle given the enormous difference between angelic travel and our own. **Psalm 103:20–21**—Besides offering Him prayer and praise, angels also do the Lord's bidding according to His Word. This includes God's will both in heaven and upon earth. Good angels are God's ministers of both service and protection, which will be detailed more fully in session six.

37. **Genesis 1:31**—God pronounced "very good" on all that He had made (Genesis 1:31). That includes the angels He had created sometime during the six days. They were holy and sinless as was the whole of God's creation. Yet God created angels with such freedom that they could choose to disobey, which some of them did. Sin was not yet present in the Garden of Eden, Satan and the evil angels had not fallen, and Adam and Eve had not yet been tempted. That changes with **Genesis 3:1**—"Now the serpent was more crafty than any other beast of the field that the LORD God had made. He said to the woman, 'Did God actually say, "You shall not eat of any tree in the garden"?'" While Scripture does not tell us the exact time when some of the angels fell, it is possible that their fall occurred through this very act of violating God's created order through Eve's temptation. Or their fall could have been immediately prior to it.

38. These passages have traditionally been interpreted as providing insights into the fall of the devil, Lucifer, or Satan. **Isaiah 14:12–15**—This passage describes the fall of the king of Babylon, but also serves as a type of the devil. In verse 12, "Day Star" is translated in the Latin Vulgate (Jerome's translation of the Holy Scriptures) as "Lucifer." Note in this passage the extreme pride of ascending above the "stars," which are traditionally interpreted as angels (v. 13), setting up a "throne" (v. 13), and becoming like the "Most High" (v. 14). The ultimate result of the devil's gargantuan pride, however, is Sheol (v. 15). **Ezekiel 28:12–19**—The king of Tyre personifies the devil, who is depicted as a cherub in the Garden of Eden until "unrighteousness was found" in him (v. 15). **Ezekiel 31:1–17**—The pharaoh of Egypt is depicted as mighty cedar tree, felled in Eden and taken down to Sheol (vv. 16, 17) with other cedars. The passage alludes to the devil's fall and the fall of the evil angels. It mentions Eden as well.

39. **Jude 6**—Of those angels who followed the devil's rebellion, losing their positions of authority in God's realm, some were taken prisoner and will be held in hell until the Last Day. Others, we learn from

other passages of Scripture, roam the earth. **Revelation 12:4**—Louis Brighton writes, "Here in Rev 12:4 the casting of the stars out of heaven to the earth dramatically portrays the dragon pulling other angels with him in his rebellion against God. A third of the stars were involved with the dragon in this rebellion. Whether one takes 'the third' as a literal number or as a symbolical number, it suggests not a majority, but a sizable minority of the angelic host. This is the only reference in the Bible which suggests the number of angels that the dragon took with him in his opposition to God" (From *Revelation*, © 1999 CPH, p. 329).

40. **Job 1:7, 2:1–2, 7**—These passages indicate that even following their fall, the devil and evil angels had access to God's throne. This access, and its later withdrawal due to Christ's ascension, will be explored more fully in answer 51, session 5, in the Leaders Guide. **Mark 5:12–13 and Matthew 12:43–44**—While these passages show incidents of demonic possession during Jesus' earthly ministry, they also show that of those evil angels, or demons, who were not bound in hell immediately after their fall (Jude 6), the remainder are loose on earth and are set in violent opposition to God, His creation, and His people.

41. **Matthew 6:10**—In the Lord's Prayer, itself part of the Christian's arsenal against the devil and his evil forces (the prayer is God's Word), we petition our loving, heavenly Father for deliverance from evil. In his Large Catechism, Luther writes concerning this petition: "Therefore, we finally sum it all up and say, 'Dear Father, grant that we be rid of all these disasters.' But there is also included in this petition whatever evil may happen to us under the devil's kingdom: poverty, shame, death, and, in short, all the agonizing misery and heartache of which there is such an unnumbered multitude on the earth. . . . So there is nothing for us to do upon earth but to pray against this archenemy without stopping. For unless God preserved us, we would not be safe from this enemy even for an hour" (LC III 114–116).

The Right Road (Connect)

42. **Matthew 18:10**—Jesus says that while they minister on earth, God's good angels "always see the face of My Father in heaven." Since sinful human beings cannot bear to even see a small manifestation of God's or Christ's glory (Matthew 17:6), this emphasizes the fact that the angels who did not fall with Lucifer are holy and do God's will. They perpetually enjoy the beatific vision of God, or eternal happiness, which we believers will enjoy only in heaven.

43. **1 Timothy 5**:**21**—Although the Scriptures do not detail of what their election consists, God's good angels that remained faithful after the angelic rebellion are now confirmed in their goodness and holiness. This means that the good angels can no longer sin, nor can they fall. They are God's own forever. This is a source of great comfort to us Christians, because it means that these servants of God always mean to do His good and gracious will for us and that they will never do us any harm. "Are they not all ministering spirits sent out to serve for the sake of those who are to inherit salvation?" (Hebrews 1:14).

The Wrong Road (Vision)

44. **John 8**:**44**—Satan did not continue to stand or abide in the truth. He turned away from God and His truth to a lie and thus became thoroughly corrupted and thoroughly evil. **1 Timothy 3:6**—In this instruction to Timothy concerning the qualifications for bishops or pastors, Paul mentions that the devil's original sin was pride or conceit, which has already been noted in other answers.

The rejection or suppression of God's truth (Romans 1:18) manifests itself in ungodliness. Pride rejects God's order and His Word (v. 20), which leads to sin. The evil results of pride were first demonstrated in Eden by the devil, then by Eve and Adam, and now by every human creature. Our only hope is our precious Savior, who came to destroy the devil's work (Hebrews 2:14–15; 1 John 3:8).

45. **2 Peter 2:4**—As noted earlier, some of the rebellious angels were confined in hell following their rebellion. **Matthew 25:41**—Because they took the wrong road of rebelling against God, the ultimate destination of the devil and all his evil angels is the eternal fire of hell, from which there will be no escape. However, those human beings who believe and are baptized shall be saved (Mark 16:16) and shall be among that great multitude in heaven crying out, "Salvation belongs to our God who sits on the throne, and to the Lamb" (Revelation 7:10).

What Do Evil Angels Do?

Objectives

By the power of the Holy Spirit working through God's Word, participants will (1) understand that the devil and his demonic angels are real, (2) see that demons can possess an individual, and (3) will know that Christ has conquered the devil and overcome evil and sin so that the final victory is ours.

Opening Worship

Consider singing "Do Not Despair, O Little Flock" (*LW* 300), "Lord of Our Life" (*LSB* 659; *LW* 301), "Rise, My Soul, to Watch and Pray" (*LSB* 663; *LW* 302), "Rise! To Arms! With Prayer Employ You" (*LSB* 668; *LW* 303), "Stand Up, Stand Up for Jesus" (*LSB* 660; *LW* 305).

Prayer: Lord God, heavenly Father, we pray that Your name would continue to be hallowed in our midst and also in the world. Restrain the devil and his evil angels. Through your Gospel, set free those trapped in the devil's lies and in the doctrines of demons. By the power of Your Holy Spirit, open their eyes to see Christ as the only true way of salvation. We ask this in His name. Amen.

Focus

46. Answers may vary. In *The Screwtape Letters,* C. S. Lewis warns Christians against undue fascination with the devil and things demonic. The fascination with evil is undoubtedly due to the allure of power, which appeals to sinful pride. Conceit was the devil's original sin (1 Timothy 3:6). Those who rely on horoscopes, experiment with the occult, participate in non-Christian worship, or play with a Ouija board delude themselves into thinking that such activities provide no ill effects. These practices violate the First and Second Commandments and are pathways for demonic influence and control.

Their Revolt (Inform)

47. **Genesis 3:1–7**—Satan (1) subverts God's order by speaking first with Eve instead of her husband (Genesis 3:1; God will speak first with Adam [v. 9], whom He created first); (2) Satan causes Eve to doubt God's Word (3:1); (3) Her faith weakened by unbelief, Eve becomes confused about what God actually said, mixing truth with error (v. 3); (4) Satan lies (v. 4) about God's Word and thus commits murder, because Eve and Adam will first die spiritually then physically; (5) Satan appeals to Eve's sinful pride, because she wants to be like God (v. 6). **Luke 8:12**—Jesus notes that the devil desires to come and snatch God's Word out of human hearts by doubt and deceit. Thus human beings do not believe the salvation it reveals and are lost in their sin. The devil "cannot bear to have anyone teach or believe rightly" (LC III 62; see also 63–64). **1 Timothy 4:1–3**—The devil attempts to replace God's truthful Word with the doctrines of demons that deceive, lie, and teach contrary to God's Word, as well as the "the commandments of men" (Matthew 15:3–9; Colossians 2:18–23), which, while sounding pious, are contrary to God's truthful Word.

48. **Genesis 3:14–24**—By participating in the devil's rebellion, the serpent was cursed. In the midst of the curse, we hear the first Gospel promise: Genesis 3:15. The woman's pain in childbearing was increased, and while equal to her husband, she would resent his headship and seek to rule over him (v. 16). The ground was cursed because of the man's abdication of his headship and participation in the woman's disobedience (v. 17). What was formerly a great joy for him, his livelihood, would now become burdensome toil (v. 19). Weeds, dangerous storms, hail, earthquakes, broken relationships, illness, disease, war, depression, death—all are the result of humanity's participation in the devil's plan to overrun and subvert God's creation. **John 8:44**—The devil's rebellion has brought deception into the world, as well as murder and death.

49. **Job 1:13–22; 2:7**—God permitted Satan to attack Job by destroying all of Job's wealth. His herds of oxen, donkeys, sheep, and camels as well as the servants who took care of them were either carried off by raiders or killed. His ten children were also killed. The devil afflicts Job with terribly painful boils, which cover his whole body. **Luke 13:11–16**—God allowed the devil to afflict this woman with "a disabling spirit" that would not allow her to walk upright or to straighten up. **2 Corinthians 12:7**—The Holy Spirit inspired Paul to describe his thorn in

the flesh as "a messenger of Satan." Paul used the Greek word for messenger, *angel*, for the demon.

When Christ taught that His followers would need to take up the cross to follow Him (Mark 8:34–38), He also included the assaults of the devil and the crosses we Christians bear. But with God's grace sustaining us, we shall gain the victory through our Lord, Jesus Christ (Romans 7:24–25; 8:18–39; 1 Corinthians 15:51–58).

50. **Matthew 4:1–11**—The devil tempted Jesus to sin by serving Himself apart from His Father's will and serving the devil, by tempting God, and finally by bowing down to the devil and worshiping him. Jesus perfectly resisted the temptations of the devil and overcame him. His death on Calvary's cross destroyed the devil's power. **John 13:2**—The devil attempted to destroy Christ's work by having Judas betray Jesus into the hands of His enemies. However, the joke was on the devil, for this is exactly what Christ came into the world to do: to suffer and die in payment for the sins of all on Calvary's cross. **2 Corinthians 11:13–15**—The devil raises up false prophets and false apostles who twist God's truthful Word. The devil can also appear as an angel of light. In this way, the devil and his evil angels turn people from the truth of God to the doctrines of lies, heresies, and false doctrines, which deceive and destroy souls chiefly by leading them away from Christ.

51. **Zechariah 3:1–2**—The devil is our tempter, deceiver, and accuser. First, the devil leads us into temptation. Then, by his lying deceptions, he leads us into sin. Then, after we fall prey to his temptations and deceptions, he accuses us of doing sin and evil. He whispers in our ears that we are unworthy of God's love, that we are such terrible sinners that God couldn't love us, nor would God want to save us. "Then comes the devil, pushing and provoking in all directions. But he especially agitates matters that concern the conscience and spiritual affairs. He leads us to despise and disregard both God's Word and works. He tears us away from faith, hope, and love (1 Corinthians 13:13), and he brings us into misbelief, false security, and stubbornness. Or, on the other hand, he leads us to despair, denial of God, blasphemy, and innumerable other shocking things (LC III 104). **Revelation 12:7–12**—Louis A. Brighton writes, "This war, this casting of Satan out of heaven, took place as a result of Christ's victory and at his ascension and session at the right hand of God [see 5:1–14]. . . . it happened when the 'Child was snatched up to God and to his throne,' that is, at the ascension of Christ. Apparently before Christ's victory and ascension, the devil could at will stand before God and bring accusations against God's saints. . . . But at

Christ's enthronement at the right of God, Satan was forever banished from God's presence and his place in the heavenly court was taken from him" (From *Revelation*, © 1999 CPH, pp. 334–336). In a footnote, Dr. Brighton mentions that although Satan continues to make true accusations against the saints, these accusations no longer stand against the elect because they are justified (declared righteous) by grace through faith in Christ.

52. These passages forbid child sacrifice, divination, fortune telling, using charms, serving as a medium or wizard, necromancy (consulting the dead or séances), false prophecy, dream interpretation, sorcery, idolatry, and sexual immorality, as well as any other occult art or pagan ritual. Christians are also forbidden from participating in non-Christian religious rites (1 Corinthians 10:14), because at their core is demonic activity (vv. 20–22). Scripture is clear that the devil desires to gobble people up (1 Peter 5:8), and that those who participate in such activities have one destination: hell (Revelation 21:8; 22:15). Unbelievers are held in bondage by Satan (Acts 26:18; Colossians 1:13). Their only hope is to repent of their sins and to believe in the Gospel, trusting in Christ's all-sufficient work on the cross, which is personally delivered to them in Holy Baptism (Acts 22:16; Romans 6:3–5; 1 Corinthians 6:9–12).

They Possess (Connect)

53. These passages indicate great physical strength, hysterics, self-abuse, seizures, and convulsions (similar to a variety of medical conditions known today), attempted suicide, betrayal of friends, and the ability to reveal arcane secrets. Generally, the following manifestations of demonic possession are recorded in the Bible: (1) superhuman strength, (2) attempts at the destruction of the human being who is possessed, (3) violent opposition to Christ and His people, and (4) multiple possession or more than one demon possessing an individual. Of course, as God in human flesh, Jesus Christ is able to overcome such demonic possession, which He does through His Word.

54. In these passages, Jesus delivered all those possessed by demons and freed them from the demonic powers that had overtaken them. In so doing, Jesus showed His divine power over the demonic powers of evil. Jesus' disciples were able to cast out demons by God's power in His Word (Matthew 10:8; Mark 6:7, 13; Luke 9:1; 10:17–20; Acts 16:16–18).

They Are Destroyed (Vision)

55. The Scriptures are clear that all who do not trust in Christ for salvation will be cast into hell for eternity, where they will suffer endless torment along with the devil and all his unholy angels. However, the only cause for their damnation will be their own sin (Romans 6:23; FC SD XI 80–81). God does not want anyone to perish but to repent of their sins and to trust in His Son for their salvation (2 Peter 3:9). Therefore, until Christ returns, the Church's constant message to the whole world is "Repent and be baptized!" (Acts 2:38–39).

56. In the end, the devil and his evil angels will be in chains, eternally tormented with fire and in the darkness of hell (the lake of fire and brimstone), which they recognize even now. The just judgment they will receive was decreed after they rebelled against God. They were reserved for judgment in hell because of their sin. Unlike humanity, they were given no opportunity to repent and to be saved. Christ did not die to redeem the angels from their sins. Rather, He came to destroy the works of the devil (1 John 3:7; Romans 6:8–11; 1 Corinthians 15:52–57; 2 Timothy 1:10; Revelation 17:14).

What Do Good Angels Do?

Objectives

By the power of the Holy Spirit working through God's Word, participants will (1) grow in their understanding of the service and protection given by God's holy angels, (2) believe that God's angels are their companions who watch over them and guard them, and (3) know that they may even have entertained angels unawares.

Opening Worship

The following hymns included here emphasize the angelic role as messengers of the good news in Christ: "From Heaven Above to Earth I Come" (*LSB* 358; *LW* 37), "Hark! the Herald Angels Sing" (*LSB* 380; *LW* 49), "Angels From the Realms of Glory" (*LSB* 367; *LW* 50), "A Great and Mighty Wonder" (*LSB* 383; *LW* 51), "Silent Night, Holy Night" (*LSB* 363; *LW* 68), "A Hymn of Glory Let Us Sing" (*LSB* 493; *LW* 149), "Jesus! Name of Wondrous Love" (*LSB* 900; *LW* 182), "Go Tell It on the Mountain" (*LSB* 388; *LW* 504), or "I Am Jesus' Little Lamb" (*LSB* 740; *LW* 517).

Prayer: In the name of the Father and of the Son and of the Holy Spirit. Amen. I thank You, my heavenly Father, through Jesus Christ, Your dear Son, that You have kept me this night from all harm and danger; and I pray that You would keep me this day also from sin and every evil, that all my doings and life may please You. For into Your hands I commend myself, my body and soul, and all things. Let Your holy angel be with me, that the evil foe may have no power over me. Amen (From *Luther's Small Catechism with Explanation*, © 1986, 1991, 2005 CPH, pp. 32–33).

Focus

57. Answers may vary. Most often we are not aware of all the things public servants, such as police officers, firefighters, hospital personnel, armed service members, and so on, do for us. We should be

grateful for the faithful exercise of their vocations on our behalf. Likewise, we often are unaware of the service and protection God's holy angels give to us. We do not see them battling evil angels on our behalf, nor do we see them warding off evil or directing our pathways in life. But these things they do for us.

Servants of the Most High (Inform)

58. In these passages, we see the extent of God's goodness and mercy being extended through the ministrations of His holy angels as they protect God's people. **Genesis 19:1–3, 10–12, 15–16**—God's angels warned and physically rescued Lot and his family from Sodom and Gomorrah, in spite of Lot's laxity in the matter, before those cities were destroyed. **Daniel 6:19–22**—The angels shut the lions' mouths, thus sparing Daniel's life and delivering him from the evil intentions of his enemies. **Acts 5:12–21**—After the apostles had faithfully preached and healed many people in Jesus' name, the high priest in league with the Sadducees had them arrested. They were rescued by an angel, who opened the prison doors so that they could preach in the temple about Jesus.

59. In these verses, we see God's holy angels do things that we may find surprising, such as executing God's judgment on wickedness and sin. The ultimate purpose of their activities is to protect God's people from evil. On the Last Day, angels will administer God's just judgment. **Genesis 19:13, 23–28**—In addition to rescuing Lot and his family, God's angels came to Sodom and Gomorrah to destroy the wicked town by raining down sulfur and fire from heaven. The resulting devastation was so great the town appeared as a giant furnace. **Acts 12:20–23**—King Herod is struck dead by an angel because he broke the First Commandment, allowing himself to be exalted as a god rather than giving glory to God. **Revelation 20:1–3**—God's angels exact God's judgment on unbelievers and the devil. This is His alien work, so it is also an alien work for the angels. Carrying out God's judgment of wrath on sin does not make God's holy angels evil or bad. God does not want anyone to perish, but to repent of sin (2 Peter 3:9) and to believe in the atoning sacrifice of His Son (John 3:16; 1 John 4:9–10).

60. God's created angels ministered on behalf of Jesus before His birth, during His earthly life, and following His ascension into heaven. An angel warned Joseph, Jesus' earthly father, to take the boy and His mother to Egypt into safety (Matthew 1:20–21); angels ministered to Je-

sus following His temptation by the devil (Mark 1:13); and an angel gave strength to Jesus following His prayer in the garden of Gethsemane (Luke 22:39–43). Other appearances of angels in the Bible during Jesus' earthly life are listed at the end of the participant session.

61. **Acts 1:10–11**—God's angelic messengers announce Christ's ascension and prophesy about His second coming to judge the living and the dead. **Acts 8:26–40**—The angel directed Philip to the exact location of the Ethiopian eunuch, a Gentile and the treasurer of the Ethiopian queen. After sharing the Gospel with the eunuch and baptizing him, the Spirit whisked Philip away for another important assignment. **Acts 10:21–33**—An angel appeals to Cornelius, a centurion, to send for Peter so that he may preach the Gospel to the Gentiles in Caesarea, which is in Philippi.

62. **Zechariah 1:7–17**—The Word of the Lord, which is Old Testament shorthand for divine revelation, is often accompanied by the presence of an angel. The angel of the Lord, quite possibly the preincarnate Christ, proclaims kind and comforting words to God's prophet. Zechariah is to relay this message about the return of God's people to the land, and the restoration of their temple. Zechariah, whose name means "Yahweh remembers," contains numerous prophecies about the coming Messiah, Jesus Christ. **Luke 24:1–6**—The angels announce the resurrection of Jesus Christ from the dead. **Revelation 1:1–3**—God revealed what John experienced in the book of Revelation mediated through an angel.

63. **Psalm 103:19–21**—The throne of God is in heaven, where angels both praise the Lord and serve Him according to His Word and will. **Hebrews 1:1–6**—Angels worship the Son of God, Jesus Christ, just as they worship the Father and the Holy Spirit, or as the Athanasian Creed says, "The Unity in Trinity and the Trinity in Unity is to be worshiped." **Revelation 5:11–14**—The angels praise, glorify, and honor Christ, the Lamb, and the Father, "Him who sits on the throne" (v. 13).

Companions of God's People (Connect)

64. Angels have particular interest in the ministry of the Church, the proclamation of the Gospel of Jesus Christ for the forgiveness of sins. **1 Corinthians 4:9**—The trials and tribulations suffered by God's apostles are a spectacle observed by both the people of this world and God's angels. **Ephesians 3:8–11**—Here, Paul notes that the wisdom of God's plan of salvation by grace through faith in Jesus Christ for both Jew and Gentile is now revealed both in heaven and on earth. Even the angels—

"rulers and authorities in the heavenly places" (v. 10)—have this wisdom revealed to them through the Church. **1 Peter 1:10–12**—Just as the ancient prophets diligently searched the Scriptures concerning the coming of Christ, so, too, do the angels desire to look into the preaching of the Church and its ways of sharing Christ with a lost and sinful world.

65. **Hebrews 13:2**—God's Word tells us that there are times when we entertain angels without being aware of it. If anything, this should teach us to be hospitable at all times.

Protectors of the Saints (Vision)

66. **Matthew 18:10**—While some interpret this verse to mean that each person has a guardian angel, at the very least we may say that God sends angels to watch after children. God's angels take special care of the children in His Kingdom. **Luke 16:22**—Certainly, if angels have looked out for us while we are living, then they will attend to us when we approach the hour of death.

67. **Matthew 24:31**—On the Last Day, when Christ returns and all the dead are raised by Christ's command (John 5:28), God's countless angels (Hebrews 12:11) will sound the final trumpet and will gather God's elect people from all over the physical world and from heaven to be with Jesus forever. Scripture is clear that the holy angels will accompany Christ at His second coming (Matthew 24:31) and that they will collect the godly and take them up to meet Him in the air (1 Thessalonians 4:17). **1 Corinthians 6:3**—Believers will eventually be the judges of angels at the second coming of Christ. **Revelation 7:9–17**—John describes all the hosts of heaven as the "great multitude that no one could number," which comes from "all tribes, peoples, and languages" on the face of this earth. The Word of God encourages us to share the Gospel with others so that they, too, would be our spiritual companions and would join us and the holy angels around Christ's throne for all eternity.

Appendix of Lutheran Teaching

Below you will find examples of how the first Lutherans addressed the topics of angels and demons. They will help you understand the Lutheran difference.

The Augsburg Confession (1530)

Philip Melancthon, a lay associate of Dr. Martin Luther, wrote the Augsburg Confession to clarify for Emperor Charles V just what the Lutherans believed. Melanchthon summarized Lutheran teaching from the Bible and addressed the controversies of the day. This confession remains a standard of Lutheran teaching.

Article XVII: The Return of Christ for Judgment

"Our churches teach that at the end of the world Christ will appear for judgment and will raise all the dead [1 Thessalonians 4:13–5:2]. He will give the godly and elect eternal life and everlasting joys, but He will condemn ungodly people and the devils to be tormented without end [Matthew 25:31–46]" (AC XVII 1).

Article XIX: The Cause of Sin

"Our churches teach that although God creates and preserves nature, the cause of sin is located in the will of the wicked, that is, the devil and ungodly people. Without God's help, this will turns itself away from God, as Christ says, 'When he lies, he speaks out of his own character' (John 8:44)" (AC XIX).

Article XX: Faith

"People are also warned that the term *faith* does not mean simply a knowledge of a history, such as the ungodly and devil have [James 2:19]. . . . For devils and the ungodly are not able to believe this article: the forgiveness of sins. Hence, they hate God as an enemy [Romans 8:7], do not call Him [Romans 3:11–12] and expect no good from Him" (AC XX 23, 25–26).

Apology of the Augsburg Confession (1531)

Philip Melancthon also wrote the Apology, or defense, of the Augsburg Confession to demonstrate, this time at greater length, the soundness of Lutheran beliefs and practices. Like the Augsburg Confession, the Apology remains a standard of Lutheran Teaching.

Article XXI: The Invocation of Saints

"Besides, we also grant that the angels pray for us. For there is a passage in Zechariah 1:12, where the angel prays, 'O LORD of hosts, how long will You have no mercy on Jerusalem?' We admit that, just as the saints (when alive) pray for the Church universal in general, so in heaven they pray for the Church in general. However, no passage about the praying of the dead exists in the Scriptures, except the dream taken from the Second Book of Maccabees (15:14)" (Ap XX1 8–9).

The Large Catechism (1529)

The Large Catechism of Dr. Martin Luther sprang from a series of sermons he preached to help his congregation understand the basic teachings of the Bible. It serves as a companion for pastors and teachers as they explain Luther's Small Catechism.

The Lord's Prayer: The Third Petition

"If we would be Christians, therefore, we must surely expect and count on having the devil with all his angels and the world as our enemies [Matthew 25:41; Revelation 12:9]. They will bring every possible misfortune and grief upon us. For where God's Word is preached, accepted, or believed and produces fruit, there the holy cross cannot be missing [Acts 14:22]" (LC III 65).

The Lord's Prayer: The Sixth Petition

"And lead us not into temptation. . . . Then comes the devil, pushing and provoking in all directions. But he especially agitates matters that concern the conscience and spiritual affairs. He leads us to despise and disregard both God's Word and works. He tears us away from faith, hope, and love [1 Corinthians 13:13], and he brings us into misbelief, false security, and stubbornness. Or, on the other hand, he leads us to despair, denial of God, blasphemy, and innumerable other shocking things. These are snares and nets [2 Timothy 2:26], indeed, real fiery darts that are shot like poison into the heart, not by flesh and blood, but by the devil [Ephesians 6:12, 16]" (LC III 99, 104).

The Lord's Prayer: Seventh and Last Petition

"But deliver us from evil. Amen. In the Greek text this petition reads, 'Deliver or preserve us from the evil one,' or 'the hateful one.' It looks like Jesus was speaking about the devil, like He would summarize every petition in one. So the entire substance of all our prayer is directed against our chief enemy. For it is he who hinders among us everything that we pray for: God's name or honor, God's kingdom and will, our daily bread, a cheerful good conscience, and so forth" (LC III 112–13).

Glossary

angel. In Hebrew and Greek, the word *angel* simply means "messenger," and in the Bible sometimes refers to human messengers. For the purposes of this study, an angel is a bodiless (noncorporeal) spiritual being created by God to serve Him and those who believe in Him. Angels possess superhuman strength and sometimes take on the appearance of human men. Evil angels are commonly called demons (see **demon**).

angel of the Lord. The phrase "angel of the Lord" appears more than forty times in the Old Testament. Where the "angel of the Lord" receives divine worship and performs divine acts, Luther and most older Lutheran commentators understood this to mean the preincarnate Son of God.

archangel. The word *archangel* appears only in 1 Thessalonians 4:16 and Jude 9. In the latter verse, *archangel* refers only to the archangel Michael. Daniel 10:21 and 12:1 also refers to Michael as a "prince" or a "great prince," which seems to indicate that only he serves in this capacity.

ark of the covenant. The golden chest God ordered Moses to have made (Exodus 25:9–30), containing the Ten Commandments, Aaron's rod, and a pot of manna. The lid of the ark was called the **mercy seat** over which were crafted two artistic representations of **cherubim**.

cherubim. Angelic beings (singular: *cherub*) that according to archaeological evidence were represented pictorially as winged creatures having a human head and a lion's body (not as winged chubby babies often depicted in Western art).

demon. Evil, fallen angels or spirits.

demonic possession. Control by a demon. The demon-possessed man at Gadara (Luke 8:26–39) displayed the following characteristics: he recognized Jesus' identity as the Son of God, had supernatural strength, and the presence of Christ caused the demons inside of him to prefer inhabiting the swine.

Devil. Term meaning "accuser." Usually a descriptive name of Satan but also used in the plural to refer to evil angels or **demons**.

Gloria in Excelsis. Latin for "Glory to God in the highest," sung by the angels (Luke 2:14). The Gloria is sung at the beginning of the Divine Service to praise God for salvation through Jesus.

guardian angel. An angel with responsibility over one of God's children (Psalm 91:11; Matthew 18:10; Acts 12:15).

Gospel. The message of Christ's death and resurrection for the forgiveness of sins, eternal life, and salvation. The Holy Spirit works through the Gospel in Word and Sacrament to create and sustain faith and to empower good works. The Gospel is found in both the Old and New Testaments.

Law. God's will as recorded in His Word, which shows people how they should live (e.g., the Ten Commandments) and condemns their sins. The preaching of the Law is the cause of contrition or genuine sorrow over sin. The Law must precede the Gospel, otherwise sinners will be confirmed in unrepentance. Like the Gospel, the Law is found in both the Old and New Testaments.

means of grace. The means by which God gives us the forgiveness, life, and salvation won by the death and resurrection of Christ: the Gospel, Absolution, Baptism, and the Lord's Supper.

mercy seat. The lid, or cover, of the ark of the covenant over which were placed two golden cherubim. Once a year, the high priest would enter the Holy of Holies, which contained the ark, to sprinkle blood on the mercy seat for his sins and for the sins of God's people. Paul uses the Greek word for mercy seat, *hilasterion*, to refer to Jesus (Romans 3:25).

polemical. From the Greek word for "battle." The term describes conversation or writing that attacks and refutes.

Sanctus. Latin for "holy," from the song of the seraphim in Isaiah 6:2–6.

seraphim. Angelic beings (singular: *seraph*), each possessing faces, feet, and three pairs of wings. The only mention of seraphim in Scripture is in Isaiah 6:2–6, where they fly above God's throne singing praises to Him.

veneration of angels. The veneration, or worship, of angels is condemned by Scripture (Colossians 2:18; Revelation 22:8–9). Lutherans honor but do not worship or pray to angels.